St. Francis
and the
Flies

St. Francis and the Flies

Brian Swann

Autumn House Press

Pittsburgh

Autumn House Staff

Founder and President: Michael Simms
Co-Founder: Eva Simms
Senior Editor: Christine Stroud
Managing Editor: Alison Taverna
Intern: Daniel Schwoegl
Fiction Editor: Sharon Dilworth
Treasurer: J.J. Bosley, CPA
Fundraising Consultant: Anne Burnham
Community Outreach Consultant: Michael Wurster
Contest Consultant: Heather Cazad
Tech Crew Chief: Michael Milberger

This project was supported by the Pennsylvania Council on the Arts, a state agency, through its regional arts funding partnership, Pennsylvania Partners in the Arts (PPA). State government funding comes through an annual appropriation by Pennsylvania's General Assembly. PPA is administered in Allegheny County by Greater Pittsburgh Arts Council.

ISBN: 978-1-938769-12-2

Library of Congress Control Number: 2015954119

For Roberta, with all my love.

Table of Contents

Part Two

{ i }

{ ii }

Part One

Images

Thrush music drifts in so rich I can't quite follow
its bent and fractured notes, the bent fractured, the fractured
bent, quick liquid rills, trills unpredictable, impeccably phrased,
precise yet impossible to remember, sung or whistled, but
recognized each time even with his trial adjustments
and yet nigh impossible to know where the song is, a trick
among trees so you hardly catch a glimpse and even then
it seems to come from elsewhere, thrown so the notes
drift to me here, lying in bed at dusk, watching lines
float across my closed eyes, trying to see what's there,
those drifting chevrons, noiseless noteless staves, magnesium
crenellations, glass crescendos unpredictable as flying saucers
that never land, so clear and almost geometric I feel I could
draw them in detail, the way the Ghent Altarpiece portrayed
an organ so clearly a working model was made from it, but
what I see could not work. What I watch is sleight of eye,
a punch line without a joke, a vigil for a ghost's shadow,
the body of an echo that's the echo itself, pain without
sensation, shape with no body, movement a kind of stasis,
darkness with no dark, the soundless song, the weakening eye
that sees something maybe meant for someone else, not me.

Cricket

In late fall a
cricket sits on
a stone beside

an empty iron
lamp, its chirps bent
out of shape the way

sky can be. It looks
like something somebody
made of spare parts for

an object that doesn't
exist, hoping it all
adds up to more

than just a cricket
tuning itself, scraping
out a few harsh

notes into the dark,
on a stone beside
the empty lamp.

Time

God didn't create the world;
he is still imagining it between dreams.
Therefore the world is perfect,

if confused, for in it time lives like
spun glass, shadows we live by,
but here it's also a mouth on which

I'll paint lips, where the wind is
generous as a river on which I'll drift
downstream past armies rotting in the mud,

past priests selling heaven, past charlatans
and celebrities, where I'll float over drowned
towns and give morning a voice that rises

and flows around rocks like figures in smoke,
threads of improvisations making day timeless.

Time of the Fieldmice

A cicada husk, crashed dragster, hole in the roof
where he'd climbed out and taken off, whistling

about the dark till calling it quits, all around
turning bare as a bombed-out airstrip with clots

of color where animals were receding to a core
at the time of the fieldmice who in lonely rooms

have already eaten most of the seeds cashed at
the bottoms of drawers, down the backs of horsehair

sofas, at the bottom of the bed you lie in, listening
to the noise stars make on very cold nights.

The House

I follow dark figures moving off under dimming
star routes until in the distance I see a house much like
the one I live in but compounded of light, almost

too bright to see. Holding my breath, I go in until
it all opens up to a space where a gnat singing as
it rises could be the first thing or the last thing left.

I stoop to pick up an apple where there are no apple trees
and feel a wing brush me where I know there are
no angels, until I see one draped in shining shadows,

hear bird song, rare as orchids, and behind it sense
the horizon piling up, the world fresh and anonymous
again, waiting to say its names, while trout flash by

my feet as if a magus had just freed them from
their bodies to turn and twist so where they begin
they end and ending begin as music among bolts of

currents quick as a thought of a thought whose song
arrives the way each star comes home when we call, and
planets float through the windows, little clicks of light.

The Stairs

I'm staring at Anna Netrebko on page five,
eyes closed, earrings falling to shoulders her

black hair cascades over. I can hear her voice
as I watch rain burning holes in snow, and see,

floating over the slush, me at my first singing
and dance lesson, the music at odds with my

movements, the teacher pushing me closer to
my partner so, touching her body, inhaling her

scent, I stumble, almost faint, break away, rush
from the room and out the door into the snow, and

here I am staring at a newspaper beside picture frames
with nothing in them. Last night, coyotes sang outside

my bedroom window. This morning I woke with one
in bed beside me, snuggled up to her hips. The carpenter

is coming today to fix the stairs. They don't need fixing.
They go nowhere, and keep on going.

The Hummingbird

Snow is falling with no more substance
than a hunch. I wake to moonlight

drifting across my face. It smells
like glass. It smells like time itself,

so now it is fall beside the pool near
the house where she died climbing

the stairs and on the calm black surface
I can trace the first stars until I see a

hummingbird on the flagstones near
my feet, and bend to pick up but a breath

blows her onto the dark water so the stars
shiver, break up, and are gone.

—In memoriam, ESM

This

hermit thrush turns dusk to
       a quetzal's tail, dawn to scarlet skeins,

 lilac, curlicues of chrome, his song
       flexible as air, bending notes like little

bars of steel beyond notation, making riffs
       of cloud-scurry that tie Plato's string in knots,

bell-notes burgeoning, sounds coming rich
       and thick in which nothing's lost, so fast

they seem simultaneous. But this "shy and
       hidden bird" is not above a yodel or high-who,

wanting me to hear, wanting me to listen as he leans
       over from the pine to my open window, before

vanishing into the woods he makes,
       the music he is

Hrafn

"...fljúga hverjan dag / Jörmungrund yfir..."
—"Grímnismál"

Before day breaks
he's already a shadow

on the snow, clipping
the porch, breaking

bits off, smashing
fences, setting off

dogs. All day he
scavenges, scats, and

night falling, takes
chunks out of any

light left, wings
fanning fires of

stars he swallows
down to their pulse

so they shine through
him and he's done, off

and flying. What's left
isn't worth having.

The Underworld

Going down past rags and bones,
past frost and roots, past
shark teeth, auricles of aurochs,
past jaws of megalodon,
through shells of murex, triton,
whelk, down among the soul's
lattices and ladders, purple sluices
and bones white as daisies, among
corpuscles among clouds of
plankton and protozoa, winds that
move trees like stags, gales whipping
across fens, rain pounding like blood
over steamy greenhouses with morphos
and satyrines, toads and ganglia
strung like lianas, leaves big as huts,
languages of clicks and tongues
liquid as heartbeats, songs of stems
and mud, grubs and microbes,
crystals and dung, and a pulse
strumming trellises of ribs, pulling
it all together where is neither
night nor day, where fingers
move in blind voluptuousness,
naked as earthworms, touching
notes from everything, here where
mind leaves fresh prints on archives,
whispers tracks onto slabs and
bedrock to bloom again and again,
here where is emptiness, the way
a shrine is important for what's
not there, here where music is
the noise silence makes, here where
a head washes up, wave-scoured,
resonant as an empty conch shell,
singing of the underworld.

Faith Sequence

"I speak to you with silence like a cloud or tree."
–Czeslaw Miłosz

{ 1 }   *Just This*

Under the whisper of Pleiades,
under intaglios and buds of blown glass

I walked until dawn brought
flowers, little bursts of intensity at

the dark's retreating edge where
water is falling over with the weight

of glass, shattering itself like time,
saying nothing, just this.

{ 2 }   *The Snow*

            builds up, silent inch by silent inch.
You hope it knows when to stop, but if it doesn't you

could imagine a faith springing up to worship it, white
its sacred color, words and melodies based on bird-calls,

unseen, never-seen birds, saving by sound alone, language
so pure it seems echoes of what's not there, reflections

substance, substance reflections, everywhere and nowhere,
as you watch all around the enveloping episteme of snow.

{ 3 }   *In Remaining Light*

Dawn creaks, wind ground-bass. Dawn grows so slow
you could wring light out faster yourself. Clouds float by

on shadows you can't fix and day passes like a wordless song.
Stones stretch, holding their breath, until it's time again

to let go, curl round themselves as the land darkens, heaves up
into mountains purple as gentians, and everything retreats

into itself, becoming what it can still believe in.

{ 4 }   *Redemption*

You, so young, what worlds do you have faith you can redeem from up there?
I ask again as he raises the flag he'd woven so it flaps its blurred hieroglyphics

in blue air supple as if in the throes of a big idea until a sudden down draft
out of nowhere tears it to pieces, scraps scattering where they fall, blown
                                                        about,

so maybe I think this time he'll come down, but no, he'll stick to his perch
though I can now see he's wavering like a slow meteor so maybe I can still

tempt him down and out of his skin thin as star-glow even if all I can offer
is the same old glass world to see with or through, or maybe he'll walk again

with me under saturated blue, past a couple of skinny trees whose few flowers
look contrived, past lizard and snake, till halted by loose strands of barbed
                                                        wire nailed

to bleached posts across which has fallen a dead saguaro over whose
                                        outstretched arms
and trunk someone has fitted a blood-stained tattered shirt all the way to the
                                                        ground.

I would like to know the matter, the result, and I would like to know where the result goes, or even if there is such a thing, for a result has to be accurate or it could keep on going to who knows where. God himself from a scientific point of view is really no more than a starting point of view, no small achievement but hardly a result. It's the same with the famous vision of "a terrible flood" the famous philosopher saw in broad daylight where all of northern Europe was engulfed in yellow waves and reduced to rubble. This was in 1913 and it never occurred to him to connect it to the political situation, as if it was free standing. Instead he interpreted it to mean that he was "menaced by a psychosis," and the outbreak of waves came as something of a relief since he was able to decide that he was going mad and so escaped the burden and responsibility of being a prophet. "God is an image," he wrote, "an image yet to come," and so capable of being avoided at least for a while. The medium of God was hysteria, he thought, with attendant spirits. Again, looking back, we can see that this was no small achievement since each spirit had a life story and even its own distinctive handwriting. He said that if your spirit is a genius you're lucky. If not you're screwed and have to start again. Luckily, we now know that you can be and go anywhere, be in more than one place at a time (a cryptomnesiac particle). You can be more than one person, each remembering the other, each making the other though this could result in a prolonged self-torment as a bodied disembodied spirit, incompatible, maybe, but not opposites, speaking a private language anyone can learn to speak. It is literature. It is about God though he is an outrageous fellow, continually disturbing, continually asking and being asked "What's the matter?" Indeed, what *is* the matter? I search for something in my life to make this true, all this, or come true, in order for it to be a result. But I still have no idea where the result goes. This is where faith comes in.

The New World

In early morning they open, pinpoints,
white, name-free, almost unseen, and

now under a sun loud as pronunciamentos,
their tiny cymbals can be heard from the

stone wall they root in, and I imagine them
as the fugitive and cloistered virtue

Milton could not praise, but as I bend down
closer I see what insects see, the world

as we first met it, before we knew it
was the world, before it was the world.

Egg

This morning on the deck, intact
and perfect as alabaster, an egg,

size of a fingernail, white.
No need to ask, since night

contains everything, even the
plump moon that squeezed through

the open window from sky's swatch
of bioluminescence, its garden

where stars sing and lie scattered
about like eggs just waiting for you

to find and ask what they are
and where they're from.

The Name

For years I never bothered to look them up, but today,
just flipping through a book, I found them, moving them

from tiny blue flowers in mats, to *speedwell,* "speedwell,"
a prayer to prosper, and so it has, this immigrant with

a Puritan name whose urge got it this far inland, up in
these mountains, living a life with me under the radar

so successfully we became invisible. But now I want to
see it, and walk out back to the stone wall that marks the

limit of my land and there they are at noon, in the wall's
shade, under the giant maple, fully open, wide awake.

For a better look I get down on one knee, go face to face,
so our world's carry across, touch in the silence of a name.

The Stone

dreams bells, small bells like showers, light undoing itself
to become an intaglio of flies on Chinese silk, sharp

wind shaking stars, nebulae over a smolder of buds,
it dreams blown glass, glass flowers in a ghost's hand,

a dragonfly hitching back-lit mica wings, taking off,
it dreams wind rising as waves rise, shaking off excess

as mist in which translucent seabirds wheel over
an ocean giving up to the shore its store of bright shells,

it dreams a single stone with sea-sheen still on it, waking to
what it thought it had forgotten, or didn't know was there.

St. Francis and the Flies

It is good to be seated in front of the flaming logs
and watch the mountains rise under the sun as flies
buzz in the corners of high panes, die and fall on me

and my book open at Bellini's *St. Francis*, his state
amicable with donkey and crane and all God's creation
where everything's in place while he stands in front

of his writing desk outside his ramada, gazing up at
the sun or singing the Canticle he'd just composed,
or even maybe looking out for flies in case they land

in his ink, clog his pen, or squat on his paper so they
force him to go against his nature and take a page
from the yet unborn St. Bernard who exorcised

a swarm of demon flies so they all dropped dead
at his holy words and had to be shoveled out of
the church in heaps. But me, I wouldn't do that.

I've trained myself to like flies. If you can like flies
you can like anything, for flies are unavoidable
as death, and as they die are replaced as if they were

all one eternal fly from the time of the god of Ekron,
Baal-zebub, leading souls from rotting flesh to purer
incarnation. And now it's night and I'm at my desk,

who knows who it is circling my goose-neck, doing a
breakdance on my book, swimming in my tea, hiding
in my hair? I could ask, the way I once asked my cat

if he was my dead grandfather and who gave signs
in the affirmative. So, as one fly lands here and looks
about, after I've lightly blown off the paper a leg or two,

a head and a few filmy wings, the way God's breath,
ruach, moved over the face of the waters, I reach for
my pen. Each fly has a story. I wait to take it down.

Beauty

I sing here in the mountains, trapped in my house, under sharp stars,
a light on, the fire burning, snow up to the windows, no one for miles,
and even if anyone could hear I doubt they'd recognize my repertoire

that climaxes with "Vilja," the soprano aria I can never manage so
I quit and I put on the vinyl. Hilde Gueden makes me cry, so I have her
sing it again, and again, a song I've loved since eighteen when the beauty

of the world was the beauty of a woman's voice, its swell and diapason,
and the closest I came to flesh was Eustacia Vye's "pagan eyes, full of
nocturnal mystery." A romantic lad, when I found out that after Wagner

Lehar was Hitler's favorite composer I almost liked him a bit, and even
felt a little sorry for Mussolini when I read that "Vilja" could have been
the last music he ever heard when, in Lago di Garda, the morning of

April 17, 1945, Il Duce said goodbye to his eighteen-year-old son who was
playing the original score of "The Merry Widow" on the piano. "Ciao,
                                                            Romano,"
he said, "keep playing," before giving a Fascist salute and getting into

the waiting car. Eleven days later he was hanging by his heels in an Esso
                                                            station.
"Such beauty," I think, rapt, gazing out the window until Hilde's voice
                                                            dying
away is replaced by a large branch snapping off loud as a gun-blast.

Thought

It might seem strange to think of hummingbirds
as I watch a snow squall. But I'm thinking
of them flying across the Gulf of Mexico and then
returning almost on cue to the place that bore them,
here where I can see one of their nests the size
of a child's fist, woven of tiny twigs, dry grass,
moss and gossamer, buffeted and bouncing at the end
of a narrow maple branch that doesn't look too safe.
I'm thinking that the only way they could be so small
and yet so tough is if, as Lawrence wrote, they were
once much bigger in a primeval otherworld
"before anything had a soul," and they'd retained
those giant appetites and abilities, now packed
into bodies a thousand times smaller, in some sort
of inverse evolution shrunk to the size of a vivid thought,
a quick insight, forbidden or guilty desires, the kind
that are bright and hot and burn you and when you try
to shake them off they fracture into spectrums that scale
and cling, ever more voracious, as poignant as obsession
whose motive is more of the same, year after year,
and so focused that when you think you're thinking them,
they've already thought you through.

The Whale

"The miniature deploys to the dimensions of a universe"
—Gaston Bachelard, *The Poetics of Space*

The village sits unfinished on my desk,
a hole in the middle as if hit by a star guided
to the spot. Power and phone wires hang.

Out of nowhere a moth comes and squats
on the church. I squeeze again into the house
on the corner with the cardboard roof,

feed the wood-stove, try to settle. The fire
flickers as the world darkens and closes in.
I think: I can't go on like this, just as I

remember the whale I once saw whose back
broke through then, with a slow heave,
shoved the sea aside and went back down

head-first, leaving little evidence he was
ever there, falling, for all I knew, forever
into the blackness, driven by a heart big

as a house, its great song traveling all over
the boundless world which another somewhere
sometime may hear and respond to, maybe forever.

Joy

Here where I stand in our mountain pasture, the wind
whistling under rocks, twisting like a dervish
round sculpted trees, these deep shadows remind me

of those in Egypt where Flaubert wrote and loved the sun
and the bronze dancer stripping to the rebecs
of blindfolded musicians, twisting like a dervish

round sculpted trees and lightly-anchored bushes,
here where I'm watching a turkey buzzard banking up
a thermal into a steep turn of sky's path, stalling,

righting himself, taking in scents clear as guiding stars,
earth's fragrant smokes rising like delight, until
he's lost in all that sky, leaving me to startled cows

as I step out into the sun, eyes shut, and find myself
free, leaping about arms beating, shirt flapping, flying,
yes, flying wordless to the wind's wild rebec.

Vega

On my bed in late afternoon I am listening
to the thrush with his song now down perfect
if not pat, and a note drawn across a tractor a mile
or more away, yes, here among scents of honeysuckle
and full-bore blackberry, wisps of bedstraw, just me, solo,
looking up at the spider crossing the ceiling constellation
then out the window where a chipmunk clucks
and a mink is running along the stone wall into
the woods, yes, here is where I would go, no need
to knock a hole in the wall to let my soul out,
the window is open so it can drift off over the beanflowers
and squash blossoms, over the worm sliding back
down after the shower, over the slug determined
to get somewhere, over chickadees in the massive
white pine, the bear digging out ants from a rotten stump,
over the turkey vultures riding the thermals into Lyra
and coyotes who bring night to life, yes, here,
in Vega, today just a general store fallen in and
boarded up, occupied for now by a young woman
who washes herself and her baby in the stream
and hides like a nymph or faun when I pass by.

A Universe

This morning I thought my armchair was on fire. It wasn't.
Just sunlight like an intense companion. And when I went out
later everywhere was still burning, slicing through the razzle

of butterflies, over clattering sparrows, baking the terrapin like
an amulet into clay, shaping the heron who stabs through
his reflection and flies off with what he's got, the leaping flash,

sunlight making the snake a gem, wrist-thick, whipping across
the path, a flick, a curl like the Pueblo sign for flowing water—
there! skin like foil, a flare through wind slicing through the red maple

and nudging the chipmunk mining the compost, finally ending up
on me filling my basket in the garden before the sun shatters
on night's shield and sheets of moiré flow in shaking out stars,

green, red, white, gold moidores clicking on night's throat,
cirrus of pearl spinning with the sound of crumpled cellophane,
swooping, centering nowhere in a laughing Lucretian universe.

Song of the Scythe

Sharpened the scythe, stroked the snathe's
rock maple curved like a spine, balanced
the grips and—down go the daisies, down
the crown vetch, clover, grass high as
a house until the thin point snags on
matted leaves, digs into a clod, bounces
out of my hands that held too tight—
don't grab, keep the heel down, step
and swing, step and swing, hold light if you
don't want to amputate a foot or lose a leg,
sweep round, go with the flow from the hips,
let the swing and sway move you on as steel
peened with hammer and jig makes its
definitive sound, the cut and crunch there's
no gainsaying or second guessing, it's final,
and the grass falls down easy and tight in swathes,
sweet hay—take a break now and then to hone
the blade with the whetstone you keep
in your belt, sound of sea on shingle, so again
the curve's a sharp frozen wave and in my head
I can't stop dancing as I look around at
goldenrod and ryegrass, wake of small saplings,
wild oats, speargrass, huckleberry bushes
that had worked their way back in, and it's
hard not to get carried away by the sway
and sweep so down go more vines and fences,
telephone poles, car, house with the shape of the gesture,
joy carrying me along as if I had an appetite
for everything and could go on forever, things
falling into place before, behind, around,
my eyes closed, letting the scythe sing
its song, its song, on, and on.

Sodden Stars

In my high meadow unnaturally sweet with thyme
the sharp-shin rang and small birds dove for cover, spooking

the horses and a deer who leaped the dry-stone wall. I watched
the hunter swoop and swerve like the Hawker Hurricane

my father made and I flew, until sky erupted out of nowhere
catching me off guard, blowing the killdeer off her nest.

Night was still too warm when I entered the lake careful
not to disturb stars, steering them aside, but they followed

like lost vowels until I got to the center, if water has a center,
when they drifted away over this reservoir of drowned towns

where I lay on my back, looking up at the turning world
in what my father called "the dead man's float," the paradox

that saved his life more than once from an oil-soaked
North Atlantic when out of nowhere, depth-charge, Stuka,

or torpedo hit, and I waited for the lake to take its time keeping
me up above where sodden stars drifted down empty streets.

Cancelled

I watch large drops hit the swallowtails, sending shudders
through their whole bodies, knocking them off maple leaves or
out of the air, and recall my father telling how he battled Nazis,

luring them into clouds, then began to gnaw another hole
in the hospital blanket, and my mother sitting at my kitchen table.
"You're not half the man your father was," she says,

not looking up from copying more aphorisms and proverbs
into the already large collection she lived by, where
each one somewhere cancelled another out.

Hero

The war over, he flew in on the feathered glory of RAF wings
stuck to his chest, and a box of medals on which was written
"What a hero. What a weight." He carried all before him, even

chasing his mother-in-law waving something she could only
describe to me years later in shocked euphemism. He bought
a second-hand MG which worked when needed, but when

his uniform didn't, he dumped it into his wardrobe along with
cartons of black-market Winstons and Lucky Strikes. From time
to time he'd take it out, squeeze into it and try his luck again

with the ladies. No go. He tried to make a go of all sorts of jobs,
but the heroes who'd stayed and manned the home front had
copped all the decent ones, so on a dark night he flew away,

and was never heard from again, leaving his togs at the bottom
of the wardrobe along with brittle packets of condoms, a box
of medals, magazines, and cigarettes that wouldn't light, being stale,

old, and damp. Years later I found him in my bedroom mirror.
You might think I'd say "Let him out. He's been in long enough.
At least grant him parole." But I don't. So there he sits in a child-size

chair bolted to the floor. I'm sorry, he mimes through the glass.
Innocent. "Oh, sure, innocent," I mouth back. We're in this together,
he replies. To myself I say: Live with it, and turn away.

Fenland Vignettes

{ 1 }   *Mail at Xmas*

The war a dozen years over, my father who fought the Nazis bravely
(though the Germans were "our brothers") has been warning me again

that the commies are coming for everything including his second-hand
Morris Minor that barely fits into his garage and once in seldom leaves.

They're welcome, I think as I pedal the red GPO bike with my heavy leather
GPO satchel through this greasy orange street light morning fog spreads

over semi-detached houses, whose house numbers are indecipherable until
you go right up and stick your nose on them at the new housing estate called

King's Hedges Road, where there are no kings, except the three I bring, and
any hedges are buried with ancient Angles in rotten fen sedge and gray mud

under rime-encrusted postage-stamp lawns, here where I wander round and
                                                                    round
on my heavy bike, lost, banging into things, bearing tidings of comfort and
                                                                    joy.

{ 2 }   *Digging Come Spring*

Heavy gray marl sticks to my spade, water seeping into the deep gash I
                                                        gouge through
rotten sedge and reeds, sucking at my feet, the old fen rising in a line we pile
                                                        near where

they'd built another council estate and found an Angle burial ground. In this
                                                        stink of

ancient air I stand up straight to breathe. "Kill it, kiddo! Kill it!" laughs Shay,

one of the

Irish navy twins, shoulders too wide to fit into the trench, posing with one

foot on the pipes

we're laying while rolling giant clay phalloi, balls to match, which he

demonstrates for

housewives who watch from behind curtains, colored scarves round their

heads, pretending

to look past us across their small dug-up lawns into the distance and its bit

of sun.

{ *Part Two*

{i}

From Oquaga

They're having fun, my neighbors,
I could curse them but this is
their life, this land is their land
on which they pursue happiness
with weedwackers, earthmovers,
buzz saws, ATVs doing wheelies
and devouring streambeds, shotguns
echoing an invasion, Coke cans
strung up and peppered full
of holes, and beyond that cars
and trucks, back and front hoes,
CATs and hammer-rigs and—
ah, a pause. Lunch, perhaps, so
now if I'm quiet and the ringing
in my ears subsides I can hear
the wind's brute history shaking
gold from trees, this old wind
blowing right at me from
down the road, from Oquaga
again with the smell of burning
lodges and the sweet smell of
scorched flesh and through
the smoke the screams of children
we've caught in the October corn
and have impaled on bayonets,
"holding them up to see how
they would twist and turn," and
their screams fill the air,
like birds in the wind.

Jesuit Relations

"Dies venit, dies tua
In qua refloret omnia"

{ - }

Autumn fires kept the land clear.
The only tall trees were on islands.
The river went suddenly slippery and jade.
On its banks eglantine and wild vine flowers
gave off an unsteady glow as the purity of the air
chilled and thunderheads heaved from the horizon,
dropping hailstones big as eggs. A spiral abyss
sucked lower clouds into its vortex without touching,
drawing the river upward with a sound worse than thunder,
any closer and our whole caravan would have made
an ascension into such sky as remained, but its own weight
brought it down. Floating groves waved in the new green chill.
The Cheyenne whose head was laid open was predicting
something we couldn't understand. Dear Father, I know
the soul's salvation lies not in description, but we can
perhaps think of all this as the new soul's description.
Many plants I saw after the storm as for the first time:
rose-colored lupine, five-petalled medicinal epinette,
and the prickly pear. The colors of the handsomest rose
are less pure and lively than the carnation of this flower.
The exterior of its chalice is adorned with all shades of
red and green and its petals evasate like the sacred lily.
It will serve us better than the rose as emblem of the
vain pleasures of this nether world. The thorns that surround
it are more numerous and it almost touches the ground.

{ - }

Night came, burning prairie to ash. Water ground
to a halt in basins, and pebbles that argue the Flood
sit in dry sockets behind us. I write this by the light

of a low flame. The demonic howls of white wolves
large as horses keep me awake as they feast on the bodies
of wild oxen whose throats we slit for tongues.
My beloved Pend d'oreilles from whom I expect much
are asleep *sub deo*. Send more to gather the harvest
of this vineyard for these poor savages are great of heart
and ardent. They glow for the Truth. Here are waiting
souls more numerous than the wild ox that cover
these great spaces like a blanket, where as I write
the faces of the sleeping savages round me glow
with the fireflies they smeared on their faces to
frighten their children. My fingers gleam with
the same wandering fire I plucked from the air.

{ - }

Bodies in buffalo robes were tied to the branches
of trees, a whole forest of the dead, where the sickness
had visited. Even the trees seemed to rot like beasts.
We had only a few old potatoes left when we perceived
a beautiful stag gazing at us, waiting for the death blow.

Billets for Bullets

Ever since they moved in it's guns all day
           and half the night.
     Rifles, shotguns, assault rifles,
whatever. But sitting at my desk, like now,
               is worst, waiting
      for the other jackboot to drop, shaking
the house like a thunderclap directly over-
           head—just now
      my heart stopped, really stopped, and I
almost fell from my chair—oh, that duo who,
            when not firing
      guns, strap on weedwackers or hop
astride a mower, a cross between a Sherman
             tank and a
      Maserati to chase down every
weed or blade of grass until they corner it,
            then, as reward,
      slip into a rubber dinghy
and race around the pond picking off frogs
            and whatever else
      is cowering in the reeds. But silence,
as I said, is worse, since then you don't know
            what they're up to,
      and think perhaps they've driven their truck
into town to freshen up their ammo
            stockpile. Big
      mistake. For if your nerves begin
retreating into place, your heart falls back
            into its slot,
      the blood begins to flow again
between pollarded banks, and the creative spirit
            gets ready to find
      its nock, then—they've got you! *Wham!*

Bam! Wham! And there is nothing to be done.
                    They're within their rights,
          the sheriff says. Get used to it.
I look across the valley to the confederate flag
                    fluttering halfway
          up the slope where the guys have decided
quiet is the better part of valor
                    and only shatter
          it when they blow up Saturdays,
or Sundays. But these two have no political
                    axe to grind—
          God forbid they should get their hands
on axes. I'd move if I could, but where to? Back
                    to the silence of
          the city? No, I'll keep on hoping,
hope the real way since hope isn't hope "until
                    all ground for hope
          has vanished," and try to finish my work
before a bullet strays across the red
                    dirt road and finds
          its billet, a phrase taught me by
my grandpa who still carried a bullet in
                    his chest "from Wipers"
          and kept another the size of a finger
in the gas mask hung up in the shed, and *ssh!*,
                    I hear a bird
          outside my window, its song reminding
me of the one I heard as a kid in the Newcastle
                    department store
          where you put a penny in a slot
and the bird on its perch in the cage began to sing
                    for as long as the penny
          lasted. It knew when to stop. But this one
seems stuck. If ever I could corner the market in silence
                    I'd give it away
          for free.

Mouse in the House

"Something tries to save itself."
                    —Ted Hughes, "Old Age Gets Up"

Now stiff is how I rise and how retire—
no, I don't mean *that*, I mean "stiff,"
as in board, and no, this is no joke, as
Dr. Lee notes, pointing to a place on the spine
he holds up which reminds me of those I saw
dangling bloody in the souks of Algiers, and
I get so absorbed I don't hear what he says,
and the pain doesn't help either, but
I thank him and try to remember what
he'd said as I walk out the door, though "walk"
is hardly the word as I move carrying my spine
gingerly while it creaks and clicks like our
old floorboards and stairs, or whatever is
gnawing through our walls, a mouse, I guess,
though at times it sounds like a hyena crunching
bones. I want to catch him before he gets to
the wiring and the place burns down, as happened
to one of my friends, but he must be as supple as
a hurdler, leaping all the traps I'd set from
basement to attic, or negotiating them like a
sapper in a minefield, though sometimes he sets
one off and scarpers with the peanut butter,
flowing like lymph into the house whose insides
he knows better than I, and sometimes when
I don't hear from him for a day or two I think
he's gone, finally taken my hints, but then,
as I sit mindfully on my sticky mat, wondering
what the MRI will find when the last one
came up empty, I think I hear him starting up
again in joist or beam, bracing, rafter, wall.

The Bird Flying Him

Pigeons burbling with tails outspread, a woodpecker
bending his beak banging away at an air conditioning unit
ten stories up, mayflower and locust giving off pheromones
and whiffs of estrogen on this first day like summer
after a winter of digging out. There is no reason not
to include them while I postpone the pleasure
of cleaning my fingernails with a sharp penknife,
though who uses pens today, after a night of scratching
and poking, trying to make amends and be forgiven in a plane
skimming rooftops, about to crash, wanting the slate clean,
because things can't wait, and it is good to plan a better future
this Earth Day e.g. up giant redwoods older than Parthenon
or Pantheon whose canopies sprout huckleberry bushes
and even other trees, who can reverse the flow of water
if they choose to put out fires in the underbrush
or back up in their heads when they catch fire.
In this other world lightning's the norm-like jolts of caffeine
which you rush to catch before it completes itself or
passes away like the long poem I wrote in my head
without words to make it new about the framers
of the Constitution based on a review of a book
in the Sunday *Times* but for the life of me when I
went back to check details it wasn't there, just books
on indie rock and reproductive rights and the like,
nowhere to be found among the "stunning tours de force"
and the like. Maybe it's hiding under the one
poetry review of a poet long dead, but no. I look
under and there's only "Major Acquisitions" on top of
Tibet and coming-of-age novels. But you can't waste
more time looking in the loam. The tree might fall,
huckleberries and all, leaves swaying in collapse, roots
neither wide nor deep. You have to push on or
fall off, swimming down at ninety mph, lungs flattening

into the small space we come from, back into our own
bloodshot eyes, the trunk becoming stone columns, fluted
to mimic origins, the wood we came from, the blood
reversed into mosaics, gold tiles, birds and deer always
representing something else, and, wings tattered, we land
in a hole, a cave, Etruscan maybe, a spring still burbling
in the prison floor like San Pietro in Carcere that held Jugurtha,
Vercingetorix, and even St. Peter, it all almost caves in on top
of Michelangelo who next door takes a hammer and smashes
the knee of Moses so what could have been we'll never know
since all that's left is Leah and Rachel, the composition
forever incomplete but complete in another way, lovely
broken scales flowing in and out, up and down and through,
like clouds of starlings Etruscan augers read from, making
another music from down among the dead to up into ecstasy,
shaping, cleaning, cutting, and still I can't find that review
of the book on the Constitution which would pull everything together.
Maybe I kept turning the page with another stuck to it
with sticky dirty fingers on hands that need more washing
the more you use them and whose nails gather mortality
I need to dig out. Or it's just not there except in my need
to have it there, my need to know how things became the way
they are and what we can do to improve them before the sap
reverses like the tide and sweeps all away, goes back
underground leaking into the dark from roots surprisingly
shallow. Maybe I could have imagined the whole thing
or it was there once for a while and never again
and is now in my mind where somehow I have the book's
synopsis and argument which I remember in fragments
because I got excited and started planning a long poem
on an important subject which would be reviewed in
the *Times* and make it to the best-seller list along with
Dan Brown, Mary Higgins Clark, and Danielle Steel.
It starts in hexameters with the Constitutional Convention
on the hot summer of 1787, hot as today, hotter maybe, with
Franklin pointing to the carving of a sun on the back
of Washington's chair and saying he doesn't know
whether it's rising or setting. The whole business was

a bit of a mess, and a wonder at the same time.
It could have gone many ways. It could, for instance,
have been hijacked by Rutledge, and it certainly
ended up cobbled together with slavery and no Bill of Rights,
shored against its ruin by later additions which I'd have
to ignore as it grew and balanced, its idealism the result
of rough bargaining by "demigods" and "coxcombs."
But then I got sidetracked by pigeons and woodpeckers
and all the rest until, flipping through a book on the Lost Colony,
I found de Bry's engravings of White's drawings, and stopped
at that man in a fur loincloth with a tasseled pouch,
a bird flying in his hair, flying him along past invisibility.

General History

> *"A doctor cannot apply medicine to the sick without understanding the cause of the sickness."*
> —Sahagún, *Historia general...*

They're building a restaurant at the top of the hill
on a street of ruined houses, glassless windows,
no doors, in front of heaped stacks of decayed cars
that never made it to the crusher, a restaurant
in the middle of nowhere still in the process of becoming
nowhere. He points it out proudly, the dentist who is
showing me around. "They're going to specialize
in desserts," he says. Open fields form the other side
of the street. And yes, I am still considering moving
into the area because I have bought a new racing bike
and want a fresh start. As we ride in his Jag
I recall riding into the Bronx on the elevated tracks, so
I tell him about the mayor who made landlords
of shattered tenements and buildings stick pictures
of flowers in jars onto the windows that remained,
or pitchers of flowers on plywood where they didn't,
one after the other. "Who did he think he was fooling?"
he asked, swerving to avoid a young driver in front
who had opened his door and was backing up, trying to
find something he'd just thrown out the window.
"How like me," I said, remembering how I once tried to
get to the Tower Bridge by bike. "What do you mean?"
said the dentist. I could see it all clearly, the bridge
in the distance, seeming to recede. Nobody could tell me
how to get there. By car, yes, but bike, no. So
I ended up in a fish market and then in a meat market
where I couldn't take my eyes off the eyes in
a horse's head lying on the stall, the severed head
that scared me in a fairy-tale ("Patient Griselda?")
where it talked and told the truth. But it's not real, it's
just a form, a substitute, I told myself, a shape, no spirit
or soul, a sculpted thing, an authorless artifact, while

over it I could still see Tower Bridge. So I dumped
the bike and jumped into a wherry stinking of fish and
floated upstream, landing among flower stalls
and garden equipment, wondering if I should steal
a packet of seeds, forget-me-nots, maybe, or change jobs
completely and instead of all this, one failure after another,
throw it all out the window. As I was thinking this,
the dentist's voice broke in with an attack on socialism
in the form of the National Health Service,
using as evidence the rotten state of English teeth.

Dame Edna, Judy Tenuta, and John Ashbery

I am on a journey to somewhere, but bought a ticket for a station
further on. I read awhile, then put down his *Selected* on the seat
next to me, and "As I sit looking out of a window" at a bit of this,

a bit of that, I watch the cozy shift of the world until I close my eyes.
Bumping along, on the back of my eyelids pictographs play on clouds,
and a collaged landscape keeps knocking into itself while trying

to avoid expectations. We've been going quite a while but we're not
even anywhere near where I thought we were going, or where
I thought we had been, so I try to hum to the train's smooth irregular beat

to pass the time. There's no schedule to keep to, though I keep some sort
of time rocking from side to side in the gently disconcerted shift
of the world and go into a deeper sleep as if breathing in oracular wisps,

a kid again, my head under a towel over boiling water in which my mother's
dissolved Friar's Balsam, inhaling deeply to clear conduits and tubes
and learn to breathe again, when my wife, still suffering from a nasty cold

and listening to Nora Jones, calls out "Hey, wake up, listen to this:
'Dame Edna has volunteered to adopt Anna Nicole Smith's daughter,
but only if she can rename her Lois. *I once had a baby called Lois,*

she said in Sydney. *It was stolen. It didn't get much publicity. I was out
and when I got back there were horrible koala tracks, giant koala prints,
and we've been looking for her ever since.'*" "Do you believe that?"

I ask. "Anything's possible," my wife sniffs, putting the newspaper
down on the seat beside her, blowing her nose and turning off Nora Jones.
"*It could happen.* Do you remember Judy Tenuta?" Do I? I love her.

Grace

First light's cold mineral glare is on this land cut over, dug out, abandoned.
On alluvial fans glacial roses push up through flag marl where ice gouged
                                                                                out

everything for moraine and esker, here where the lake turns to the luster of
                                                                            chert
loons who dip, pause, and vanish, here where loess has filtered into the lungs

of scrawny trees whose breath I breathe, here where a wind-blown
                                                            rock-flower
roots deeper than jackpine whose laterals slip off stone, here where on
                                                            bleached bones

lichens hunker, moss leavens, and ore locks in our blood while the sky
                                                            reaches
down, backs off, leaving glare, tailings, the gloss of grace.

The Heroic

Here where land was dug from swamp and sea, balloons rise,
silent annunciations going the wrong way. Someone shouts
from a hole in the sky. Rain falls. When night falls
it brings dim stars and a slit moon, and I find myself
thinking of Rembrandt's one-eyed Batavian king
with his band of grungy revolutionaries swearing
a sword-oath, of those who go against the grain,
tell the truth and pay the price, the old master
cutting up his masterpiece the city fathers rejected,
leaving only a fragment to torment us. All care
about heroes, the self-possession, the rage like rocks
between the teeth, so why as I cross canals tame
and acidulous do I see rise in the dark California,
where I've never been, lemons ripening, long gardens
where mulberries hang and air's elastic, where you
can say to yourself there are so many ways to be
happy and monumental at the same time, where girls
dive into waves like seabirds and come up somewhere
out of sight, forever anonymous, untroubled, young?

Continuo

Albinoni's Adagio in G minor for strings and organ continuo,
a line of washing waves in the morning breeze from Ostia as a
girl-child moves slowly down a circular staircase from the roof
into the half of the courtyard still in shadow, Albinoni, a palazzo by a canal,
arabesques over the water gate, a merchant's sign over voluted windows,
a dromedary with a large load, and lost in rain sweeping in over
from the Laguna Morta the sounds of carpentry, some comfort in the scent
of wood and sawdust, and in the hill-fort near the chalk-pit where we
gathered fossils they found in a corn-drying pit a sack still
secured by a single bronze needle and inside that a girl about six,
legs severed and head missing, and in a rubbish pit a woman
about forty with crushed pelvis, lying beside the burnt bones of a horse,
and when I was five Lancasters and B17s dropped hell on Dresden
where now a replica Baroque skyline is rising so time is unhinged
and history never happened, and while I watch a mink with a chipmunk
limp in its jaws run across the road where the week before
I'd seen a catamount they say no longer exists here just as they said
the wolf I'd watched in the woods behind my house was extinct,
while the Victor's cockpit had dug itself into a cornfield
after the crash with the Canberra, bits of both scattered everywhere.
A holly tree had burned but not much corn. No survivors. It all looked posed
as I drove through the Devil's Dike to the Wash, just after the Russians
invaded Czechoslovakia, and the TV said now they will have lost
the confidence of the Afroasian bloc, just as I did when not long ago
I found out that Albinoni's Adagio in G minor for strings and organ continuo
which I'd loved and counted on was written by Reno Giazotto in the fifties,
but at least the lovely "Dresden Amen" that had haunted my skull since
choirboy days now had something like its old home back in the reconstituted
Frauenkirche whose model had been Venice's Santa Maria della Salute
where as I tried to pray I had my wallet lifted and my watch slipped
off my wrist. "Ah Ah Ah Aaah-men."

Concerning the Infinite Universe

There is the swell of a diapason, collapsing
into everything, collapsing everything into moonlight
over the Forum I can't see from my window
but know it's there. Everything's alive.
Gray smooth cobbles answer as if the narration
wasn't in question. The invisible is everywhere.
The question is how to see it. For instance,
I live in the ghetto. There's nothing in my room
on the Via del Tempio except a camp-bed.
We have yet to be evicted and the starlets moved in.
In the bathroom a bath piled with unwashed dishes,
moss in the sink constantly dripping like the
dairy walls when I was a kid, a window broken
all the way to Ostia, wine bottles cluttering
the balcony. Why stay inside? I sway down
in the open cage in the dark (five lire in the slot),
drawn back to the almost empty Campo where
they stole everything I owned when I moved
cross-town and set my cardboard suitcase down
for less than a minute. I'd put out word the papers
were worth something to me, so I got a few pages back
caked with fine Tiber silt. Now in the Campo I can still
see the same moon Giordano Bruno saw in his
multiple universe, but this time it's above his head
and it is only like a fire—they burned him upside-down,
appropriately, maybe, since he'd said there is no
absolute up and down. Naked, his tongue was
in a gag. Now there is fruit rotting at his feet
and petals sweating underfoot. Vespas still zip.
The heat's still on, like a plot without a story,
as it is here where I'm trying to make out
what a tinny female voice is saying on the intercom
to the Catskill work crew who've been rebuilding

our dirt road for two weeks now with huge machines
that shake the ground so I feel the house about to fall
into the valley. All they do is rip up and smooth out
and roll flat, recycle, no new stuff. How appropriate
since thirty years after, I'm re-reading
De l'infinito universo e mondi.

Narratives

"Narratives are one sort of trace we leave on the world."
–Gary Snyder

"Stand in front. Here, hold my bag." She reaches
                    under her skirt. Digs a hole
with her heel in the gravel of the taurobolium.
Buries it. "Joining all the blood down here,"
          she says.
                              Upstairs, on the way out,
          she rinses her fingers in the basin by San Clemente's
great doors. "They were all over the city," I say.
                    "Churches were built over them."
"Tertullian says Mithras was invented
by the Devil to mock Christ." "More like
                    the other way round." "That's history for you.
One big *puticolo*."
                              By the time we get
to the Largo Argentina for a 64 bus
                    the sun is overhead. Where Caesar
was stabbed in Temple C a cat is licking himself.
"Do you think that's where we get the word 'understand'?"
                    she says. "You stood—" "Not you. Men only."
"You stood-under the grill and the blood of the stabbed bull
poured over you and you under-stood. Immediate,
                    unmediated transformation.
No blood of the lamb there. It's certainly something
you'd remember." "All I remember from
                    last night is too much Frascati, three
          young nuns dancing, and we were in love." "Still are."
The bus comes at us like a chariot out of the sun.
                    On board I say, "Remember Rtis
          in the chariot leaning down and saying to Mithras:
'Step up closer. Bend down'?" "I do." "And as he does so
                    his loose Mede trousers ride up. Rtis embraces him
          and says, 'You have such handsome calves.'" "They marry."
It's the wrong bus but somehow we still arrive

at the Vatican. "It says here St. Peter's
was built over a cave." "Mithras," I say.
"He was everywhere." "This place is too big and too much.
It tries too hard." "Somebody said
it would make a great bronchitis hospital for those
with delicate lungs and delicate fantasies."

"I prefer the solar bull to the pale
Galilean," she says. "The world has grown gray from
his breath."

We get another wrong bus and walk
back home through the Campo de'Fiori. She
pats the base of Giordano Bruno's
statue, where he burned.

That night, on our balcony
in the ghetto, we stand looking up over the city's
lights at the sky's coronal loops, the power
of each part of sunlight. "All those stories
in the sky. Who's your favorite?" she asks. "You mean
the magnetic field of the sun's fusion,
the pure force of the Milky Way, the inner
necessities of the Virgo Clusters? Do you know
that 'myth' and 'mouth' are related?"
I say. "It makes sense," she says, "but I'm
not sure I like your latest story." "It's not mine.
And it's not really a story. It's science."

"How can you tell science it's got nice calves?" "You can't.
And who would want to anyway? There'd be
no point. It wouldn't understand."

Da Volpini

"...lurking disembodied in the memory grotto..."
–Philip Roth, *Imagination*

We're worming our way into the fifteenth century
            grotto-cavern under
the house where St. Ignatius Loyola lived.
"Just one glass" begins the ritual as Volpini
            starts to slide open the
huge door a bit and blinks. "Just a taste.
            Then you must go. I'm c-
closed. What if the p-police find out?" We
squeeze in to find the cobbler, an ex-bandit from
            Sicily, walking around
with his brother, whispering. They nod, then
            leave. "Brolio?"
"Why not?" Volpini vanishes, returning
with a bottle, and his stutter, more a stiff
            crick of sound in
his throat that lands on the lips of terracotta
            oil jars under
a wall plaque for his grandfather from
the College of Vintners signed by the Pope in 1856,
            as light from one 50-
watt bulb gleams off the bald pate
            of the seventy-year-old
virgin where Pope Pius X had patted
his boy's locks after a nun had swatted them. He
            holds the bottle up to
his eyes and stares, enthralled by the mold
            on top of the cork. He
sets it down, takes his penknife out,
cuts round the top as if making a graft, takes
            a corkscrew, works
it slowly in, pulls it gently out
            just to loosen, moves
the cork side to side with his fingers until

it just slips out. "Mmm," he says. "Just look at it.
                    The cork is pu-u-urple. Beautiful.
              58. Smell. Mmmm." He pours it into
                    beakers and hands them round,
              refusing one himself because he says
he has to go to supper at his sister's, although
                    he knows we know he's
              not, that he'll sit here till midnight counting
                    his money, dipping his fingers
              into the water on the saucer beside the Chianti
flask on the marble-top table. But slowly he
                    relents and says he'll have
a *ditto*, so I put a long finger alongside
                    a glass and pour as he
              protests. We know what comes next. He shuffles off
into the dark and returns with a tin which he opens
                    slowly to reveal
              bedded on tissue a cigarette Anthony
                    Armstrong-Jones gave him
              on a visit incognito with Princess
Margaret. "Talking of which," says Edward, "today's
                    the *onomastico*
              of St. Edward the Confessor." Yael says
                    his name means Michael,
              which sends Volpini off for a calendar which
he riffles through confusing the Michaels, the saint of the angels
                    with the archangel, while
              telling us the story of the Roman fisherman
from the ghetto here who caught a huge fish which
                    Ottavia, wife of the
              emperor, saw from the palace window which
                    site is now occupied—
              he starts to draw in floor-dust when *Knock! Knock!*
Enter two polizei, one in blue, the other in
                    green who wish us all
              good evening as Volpini hands them
                    two glasses and pours while
              the one from Pompeii extols the virtues of

Vesuvian wine and the Tuscan says his wines can't
        be beat. "It's the soil,"
he says. "Sun," says the other. Volpini says
        it's Eduardo's saint's day,
and they toast him. "Auguri! Auguri!" As
they leave they tell us to drop by their barracks any time
        for a glass. Volpini
    says now we must go, but we want to discuss the
        virtues of Vernaccia.
      "Mmmm," he says, and goes for a bottle
which he holds against the bulb. "Ver-er-naccia," he whispers,
        and from the label reads
      "Aiuta il lavoro p-psichico e
        le rea-realizzazione
    artistiche..." I buy it, the Sardinian
green-gold, 700 lire, and set it down
        later to toast on
    my own the principessa from Bologna
        the three of us had
    stayed with several days, sleeping in
the same bed until she threw two out and kept
        me to tell her story
    to, underground anti-fascist work,
        capture and torture, how
    years later she went mad and in the cinema
everyone moved away from her before she realized
        she'd stuck chicken-parts
    up her cunt and lettuce up her ass,
        so she ran home and
    threw all her dishes out the window till
the police came and she spent a year in a rest home,
        and then I think of
    the exercise mistake a student at the Magistero
        made turning "We stayed
    at that woman's house for several days" into
"That is the house whose woman we stayed in for several days."
        And then we leave, Yael
    still upset about the death of Che,

who will later leave
for Sweden, where Mossad will hunt him down,
and, they say, in a case of mistaken identity, kill him,
and Edward, on the run
from Nam until his liver caught up with him,
and me, "lurking disembodied in this memory grotto."

Perspective

"...and make it move and live..."

I'm staring at pictures of the walls
                    at Pompeii's Villa dei
          Misteri which, it says, are rubble core
sandwiched between plaster so
                    they breathe, and the earthen
          pigments breathe too with Dionysus and
animals and panpipes, the young
                    woman in a swirling
          cape, a ritual flogging underpinning
the trance of transition, and my mind
                    slips to Coleridge also
          on my desk, his school floggings and
humiliations, hedged by terrors
                    at his fate of copy
          clerk or conscripted sailor, my fate too
if my father had had his way,
                    hence the need to succeed
          by any means at all, drugs, plagiarism,
vision or trance, to battle dejection
                    and balance himself, train
          the eye to see what isn't there, the way
Bernini at the Vatican
                    was given two small
          mean stanzas and told to make one grand gallery,
and so he cheated with stone tapestries,
                    heavy and brocaded,
          lifted by stone cherubs, and on the royal
staircase gave the impression of slow
                    majesty by long
          steep stairs, bringing pillars in with false
perspective. This was the same Bernini
                    who at age fifteen
          while sculpting St. Lawrence had put his own leg into
the fire to observe the expression of true agony.

Slugs

I prayed for rain and rain it did.
The moon brought the rain but
the rain brought slugs. I did not pray
for slugs. My neighbors say the rain

makes slugs the way rotting meat
makes *mosche*. What use are they?
"The law cannot be known properly
by thought and discrimination," says

the Lotus Sutra. So I try again. Looking
close, they seem relaxed and easy-
going in shades of orange, brown, gray,
some striped, some fat as my thumb.

They can give you a nasty bite, my
neighbors say. They've bitten you?
I ask. Not yet, they say, and piss on them
until they shrivel up. But I try to see them

in a different way, pebbles in a Zen garden,
helping attain no-mind, non-attachment,
no judgement. Now even the word
"pebble" makes me feel better about them.

So I try working with Shiko's koan of the earth-
worm he cut in half while hoeing and asks
which half has life but it turns out somehow
to be about the hoe, which could be the

creative mind. In any case I keep on trying
on behalf of slugs which is, of course, on
my own behalf since I do not wish to know
the world like Audubon by stopping it. But

no one has a good word to say about slugs,
and as I watch them heading out in
morning's cool to bring my Eden down,
"plant, fern, and flow'r," I try recalling

the bestiarists who found a use for them.
But I soon quit and, taking a page
from my neighbors' book, making due
allowance for wind velocity, gauging parallax

and calculating vectors, arcs, and angles,
taking careful aim,

World's Shadow

On my adobe's red-earth floor something is making the light jump
like a jack rabbit, up and off whitewashed walls. The flowers outside
take in canvas or run it out, stretching their brightness to morning's
indigo which they breathe in and turn glassine, and I think: things are

only so deep, emblems of rhythms not the rhythms themselves, hints
to pick and twist to other dimensions the way those buzzards are rising
out of sight in wide baldacchinos following air's grains, while round them
gray skeins draw down and across to form the skyloom the Tewa say

the world is woven on. The rain is still in distant mountains as the sun
breaks free and tries to stand alone, then begins to move toward me,
drawing cloud-threads into a lovely tree that flickers and unfurls.
It's a trick, I know, as I watch it spread into a huge bole and branches

draped with Spanish moss, but hanging from a bough by his neck is
a black man, a doll in the photo I found as a child, a marionette that still
stays on that tree twisting, an ornament bloody and unsexed, as worshipers
look up smiling, posing for the camera, men women and children my age

at their world's renewal, so I close my eyes, trying to trace the lovely tree
climbing from the earth over sage and creosote bush, up into the world
of faded star-bones, into the icy vastness whose shadow this world is.

At Tlalocan with Yma Sumac

From my window more windows, more frames,
      no blue, just glass, cordoned, confined, and reflections
      of blue and sometimes white or gray, and when night comes
it makes everything night, sucking up any color and turning it
      splotchy, yellowish, in patches, to go with the black that keeps
      building up and slipping off in flakes like skin, and behind
the glass people watch TV's unearthly light and dream. Or not,
      or do things, or not, like working out on a treadmill
      that doesn't really work and jerks along, and stops, though
why I imagine a treadmill I don't know. Maybe I should have them
      doing yoga, except nobody round here does yoga unless maybe it's
      Octavio Paz, and he's dead, or unless it's because I write
fast with a pencil that goes where it feels like and treadmill means
      something special to it, like this famous Swiss writer I read about
      who used "the pencil method," its rhythmic flow, the rhythm
of reverie, the "unique bliss" that calms you down and
      cheers you up, slipping over the page's white ice,
      cutting figures you had no idea you knew or even knew
were there, and that's how they found him after he'd
      gone insane, frozen in a field, cutting his own figure
      on his back, sprawled in the snow, all he had to
fall back on, eyes wide open as if still trying to see,
      mouth agape, as if still forming a phrase, though the hand
      that held the pencil was a claw, like Big Foot's at Wounded Knee,
his world gone with him forever, taken, never to return,
      the world where everybody talked, animal, tree, stone, us,
      as easily as the way birds slip through air, expand and link the air,
make it thin enough to move through, thick enough to glide on,
      where you can see further and further even when you know
      so little and can say even less with hands stiff from rheumatism
and a right metatarsal thick from gout, punishment for gluttony,
      double comic because I eat little. I wonder: When
      you're reborn from this place are the hands healed

and is the big toe and the other parts reborn like a baby's,
cool and placid as the swans that swim like clear ideas on the lake?
"Can anything satisfying be found on earth?" sang the prince
Nezahualcoyotl, which sounds a bit petty for one who had it all.
"Wait it out, señor," said the doctor when I told him I couldn't pay.
"This too will pass." Pretty good advice, I suppose, that fits
about anything, one way or the other, even here in Tlalocan in the rain
where the buses from the springs of Chapultepec and all points
beyond,
red, black, white, blue, pull up and let out the various
drowning victims, those with legs and ankles swollen with dropsy,
fellow hobblers with gout and those lightning struck down
on mountainside and golf course. If you photographed this place
in the valley, aside from the willows and waterbirds, the accustomed
and conventional green corn, squash, sprigs of amaranth, green
chiles,
tomatoes, string beans, flowers and quetzal plumes, you'd get
a foamy effect, like detergent, a glittering like fish scales, a flickering
like fireflies on water thick and opaque as isinglass. And if the
camera
could run backwards to before I even got here it might also show
me
planning at least in my mind to train eagles to hunt iguanas
in the Sierra Madre after I'd counted on the draft to be a hook
to snag on, catch me falling, except the board made me 4F, or later
after the one review of my only novel to date, the one that said
my characters (which I'd carefully drawn from life) were like
fairy-tale creatures whose world had ended and who couldn't cope
with "the real world." "Real world"! But it might also catch me
arriving here because I'd heard that the wondrous liquid
Yma Sumac was from these parts and I wanted to get to know her
in her natural habitat. It turned out, however, that she was either
an Incan princess, as she said, or Amy Camus from the Bronx,
as the papers said. And in any case, she wasn't from hereabouts
and I haven't met her, yet.

Off the Pan-American Highway

I can still see myself looking up at Shirley Jackson's widow's walk
         in Bennington and thinking how thin the modern veneer
         even though it was only a story and though it takes more
of an effort nowadays to imagine the mind behind the knife
         that gave to Tlaloc the baby born with a cowlick, and
         even if we understood, what then? The priests were
virtuous men. And I was being virtuous and civic minded when
         I made a compost pile at the bottom of a tall tree
         in the park of derelicts and druggies since it would later
help feed them from my garden, especially since the tree
         was protected by padding almost to the top, like an
         Aztec warrior. But when I went to the town hall to ask
them to keep an eye on it they said nothing could be done.
         So I just had to watch as kids piled up tires and
         old mattresses and wood so it looked like a
Guy Fawkes bonfire and when the garbage men arrived
         they picked up some and set the rest on fire,
         rich compost and all, the stench woke me up with
a terrible hangover in the hotel room of a town I'd
         arrived at by chance pulling off the Pan-American
         Highway at nightfall and thinking it was somehow all
my fault they'd hung up by their feet those three thieves,
         strung them up like Mussolini from that big tree
         with white blossoms, gagging them first, then beating them
like piñatas so bad the blossoms were red, and castrated them
         and set them ablaze, still alive and squirming like hooked fish,
         while the fiesta continued all night and the smell of burning wood
and flesh hung over the dancers, mingling with festive smells,
         and women danced with women, mothers with daughters,
         aunts with nieces, grandmothers with granddaughters,
each in a full white dress over petticoats and lace, white
         blouses embroidered with flowers like a garden, gold
         jewelry, all beautiful and looking like Frida Kahlo and as I

walked around that morning nobody could tell me
what the fiesta was all about or why it was called "Vigil"
unless it was because no one slept and who could sleep
on such a night and nobody knew anything about three thieves
so I thought maybe I'd had too much wine and had read
"The Lottery" one too many times, until I came to the plaza
and a scorched tree, dark splotches on the grass, and as I walked
about, other trees, and patches where no grass grew.

The Star Husbands

The night sky was so sharp and insistent I forgot
I was here or anywhere.
This is what I'd worship, this
"resurrection of presences," this is what
I'd want to keep going,
by blood if necessary, rather
than the pure brute fact of the sun. I tried
to call them off the
lamp-lit veranda, to come out,
it was something seldom seen from these
volcanic slopes so often
misty, the sky filled with water
droplets, smoke, or dust. But they kept talking,
bits reaching me—"...and they
used to say *los indios no*
oigan por las nalgas...and..." I try
again. "I've seen it before,"
called out Lucinda, "near Montreal"—
a jab. She'd known my ex. But why my need
to share? Proof, like counting
coup? Proof you exist under
so much vacancy? So I stood beside
the jacarandas and broken
lemon trees looking up
and didn't feel lonely, thinking that to them
up there I too could be
a spark in a dark firmament,
and again I called, asking them to douse
the lights, if only for
a moment, and come out with me here,
but they didn't hear and so I walked further
into the dark looking
up and falling about, the mind

up and falling about, the mind
emptying, punctured words escaping—*shack,*
                    knife, clone, rope-a-dope,
        and more, stars ringing, stuttering, clicking
in place, moving about, settling down
                    into lines, whorls, shapes with no
        narratives, in an unknown syntax but
singing with light, and I lay on the tired soil
                    that once uttered sugar's sweetness
        and as I lay remembered the story
of the two young Indian girls who lay down on
                    their backs on a night such as this,
        looking up at the stars deciding
which they'd like to marry until two handsome
                    youths arrived and carried them
        off way away where it was too late
for them to change their minds and in the version
                    I recalled they never returned.

Lost in Translation

They're talking of Pedro, the name, the rock on which
    a church was built based on a pun, and how mistranslation
    gives us "virgins" in the Muslim paradise instead of "sweet raisins,"
And how "young woman" becomes "virgin" and another
    religion is born, and how a lost translation of buried
    gold tablets produces those young men in gray flannels,
White shirts and knotted ties who come out to save us
    even on days hot enough to melt water, save us
    from rooms like this where the sweet smoke is locked in
And passed around and where I open the window
    onto the street. My visitors this evening include mole-eyed
    middle-aged lawyers from Valle de Bravo whose kids are
Fresas, strawberries, who do lines on 10-lire bills and go
    "to the desert" for the divine flesh of mushrooms.
    Flower-scrolls flow from their mouths, the intoxicating
Flowers that could be morning glory, *ololiuqui*, the same seeds
    kids in college chewed and then flew off the roof past my window
    and onto the grassy courtyard and the emergency room.
The light goes out and night is set in motion
    as a marquetry casket. I hear music, the entanglements
    of insects, the dark opening onto a place where
The desert cools. "There is the courage to exaggerate,"
    says Angela. "Why does the body confine itself to truth,
    or clothes?" One day, I say, I will take all you say into consideration.
But then I will leave like the Franciscan down the hill to seek
    even more deprivation and humility. Angela says she's
    an artist and tells the story, again, of Courbet in the
Sainte-Pélagie Prison painting Paris from the top floor the way
    he painted his seas, as if everything was the movement of waves.
    So, I say, he saw everything the same way. How useful is that?
Streets are no sea. They suck you up. "To heaven?" she says. I say
    there's a confusion of genres here. I will call this *song*,
    so there's nothing to prove. "Do you know the story about the reed
                                         mat?"

so there's nothing to prove. "Do you know the story about the reed
mat?"
Says "Conejo," the English teacher. "The coiled snake, the live deer
and the bird hatching eggs? It's all about power. Or," he adds,
"the story of the Pope aiming his blowgun from the Place of
Willows,
At the roseate flowers and butterflies shining like the wind, the jade wind
blowing through cacao flowers?" Nope, I say, but I have just read
about the Chief of the Federal Police who used to live in Culiacan
and who
Was killed after he arrested Osiel Cárdenas of the Gulf Cartel. "They own
us all," said "Conejo." "The chief was my uncle." Then he adds,
"meth
is easy to make." I thought he said "myth" and was about to
disagree
When a pick-up shot by, AFI officers in black, machine guns, flak jackets.
"They just wait till they leave," says Angel. "And then they come
back out."
They're heading north where the city has dried itself up. I can see
them
In the Chichimec desert, among dust, arroyos and rocks, everything
suspended
in its own time, becoming light that goes in spirals, moving about
not touching the ground, fragrant in its own way, turning into
more
of what it is, melting the way a fish in fear of its life turns into water.

Notes & Acknowledgments

"Off the Pan-American Highway": Some details are from Alberto Ruy Santez's essay, "Visit in Tehuantepec," *Creative Nonfiction*, 23, 2004.

"The Star Husbands": Octavio Paz once wrote that poetry is not truth but "the resurrection of presences," and that it is "the apple of fire on the tree of syntax." "Los indios no oigan por los nalgas"/ "Indians only hear through their backs," i.e. by whipping. A reference to the old hacienda and encomienda systems.

{ - }

Some of the poems in this collection have appeared, sometimes with different titles and in different versions, in the following journals:

American Scholar: "Lost in Translation" and "The Underworld"
Boulevard: "Egg" and "The New World"
Cincinnati Review: "The Whale" and "The Stone"
Cumberland River Review: "This"
Gettysburg Review: "General History" and "Dame Edna, Judy Tenuta, and John Ashbury"
Hopkins Review: "Billets for Bullets" and "Cricket"
Hudson Review: "Joy," "Time," and "Cancelled"
Iowa Review: "Narratives"
North American Review: "Perspective"
Notre Dame Review: "The Bird Flying Him," "Concerning the Infinite Universe," "Da Volpini," and "At Tlalocan With Yma Sumac"
Plume: "Vega"
Paris Review: "Jesuit Relations"
Poetry: "Slugs" and "Time of the Fieldmice"
Poetry East: "From Oquaga"
Poet Lore: "Hrafn"
Sewanee Review: "Sodden Stars"
Salmagundi: "Beauty" and "St. Francis and the Flies"
Southern Review: "Off the Pan-American Highway," "The Star Husbands," and "Hero"

Southwest Review: "The Name"
Western Humanities Review: "Continuo"
Yale Review: "The Heroic," "Images," "Thought," "World's Shadow," and
"Fenland Vignettes"

The Autumn House Poetry Series

Michael Simms, General Editor

• Winner of the annual Autumn House Poetry Prize
Coal Hill Review chapbook series

Design and Production

Text and cover design: Kinsley Stocum

This book is typeset in Bell MT, a Monotype font designed by Richard Austin and the Monotype Type Drawing Office. Monotype's hot metal Bell series from 1931 was based on original types made by the punchcutter Richard Austin for the foundry of John Bell in the 1780s. The digital Bell closely follows the design of the hot metal 18pt version, and is therefore somewhat lighter in color than the text sizes of Monotype's original metal face.

This book was printed by McNaughton & Gunn on 55# Glatfelter Natural.